£10

Girls o

Rosemarie Rowley

GIRLS OF THE GLOBE

ARLEN
HOUSE

Girls of the Globe

is published in 2015 by

ARLEN HOUSE
42 Grange Abbey Road
Baldoyle
Dublin 13
Ireland
Phone/Fax: 353 86 8207617
Email: arlenhouse@gmail.com
arlenhouse.blogspot.com

Distributed internationally by
SYRACUSE UNIVERSITY PRESS
621 Skytop Road, Suite 110
Syracuse,
NY 13244–5290
USA
Phone: 315–443–5534/Fax: 315–443–5545
Email: supress@syr.edu

978–1–85132–117–9, paperback

Typesetting by Arlen House

Cover image:
William Holman Hunt, 'Claudio and Isabella', 1850

CONTENTS

Acknowledgements are due to the editors of the following publications in magazine or online where some of the poems, or versions of them, first appeared:

Boyne Berries, Cork Literary Review, Crannóg, Ecozon@, Green News, The Irish Times, Leitrim Guardian, Literature Today, Mediterranean Poetry, News4Plus, Mezzo Cammin www.mezzocammin.org, Poetry Ireland Review, Poets with Voices Strong, Poethead, Poetry Porch Sonnet Scroll, Poetry Soup, Prose on a bed of rhyme, Riposte, Southword, Tiger Tiger, York Mix sonnets.

I would like to thank Professor Maurice Harmon who read many of these poems, and those friends who encouraged me through various drafts, Margretta Desmond, Mary Guckian and Dawn Sullivan. Special thanks to my son David for coming up with the title and to Siobhan and Amy for inspiring me to continue with my work and everything else.

GIRLS OF THE GLOBE

VIOLA

Androgyny is the pier glass of this caper
By playing other I will catch my love
For not all is true that's writ on paper –
There are no sailboats in the sky above:
A quick tack mummery of a daily show
Can make me and my manner most quotidian
But when midnight comes I'll go the way I go
None can deceive the blood meridian
To song and revel I'll bestow my blessing
Outlast the tragedy of mere appearance
Which as we know is only window dressing
After night time's flute comes day's forbearance
All lies for love, and love is all that lies
Within our compass and with all disguise.

ROSALIND

All hearts are true if given but the chance
To live inside the forest deep of Arden
And carve a name on every tree perchance
It is the fairest in the living garden
All love surrounds me, name and fortune match
And true love lightens us beneath the skies
I am no wanton that the fairies catch
Can be everything, yet with no disguise
My heart is plain and beautiful as a flower
Clothed more gloriously than Solomon of the Bible
No tricks enhance this nature's power
Where simplicity and beauty both are liable
To tune the heart till it bursts with joy
That Rosalind has found her lovely boy.

PORTIA

If she were able to lie, yet discern
From appearance a truth held up in court
Her lawyer's robes a costumier's to learn
The difference between a crime and a tort;
The world would not be quite divisible
And flesh and blood no concourse of shame
In which feelings were quite invisible
And *trompe d'oeil* called by another name
The misdemeanours on this lover's quest
Would be the subject of a civil action
In which surface would be second-guessed
And wig not given any other traction;
If women ruled in law without disguise
We'd all be better off without the lies.

PERDITA

Banished because of a testy father's rage
Your life is precious to your faithful mother
Your presence scarcely registered on the page
Yet you and she never found another,
You would be there as a mere ephemera
Your absence signifying patriarchal guilt
On the imagined coastline of Bohemia
Where nature flourishes, and nothing gilt;
Yet only art can rescue the act of stealth
By which you became exile, like a tree
Turned from a god's pursuit of wealth,
As beautiful Daphne was chastened, to memory;
So you're in the story, the king in the last round
Vanquished; where you, once lost, are finally found.

OPHELIA

If she were freighted in gold, in a splendid barque
In which to log her passion and her pledge,
If she could see beyond the windless dark
Of her lover's despair, and not go past the edge
Of fruitful discourse, if she had met
His pleas with rendered accounts of joy
He would be hers, her own: not yet
Remembered as a timid, rancorous boy –
A quest for others, his father's ghost to trace
In the covert coven of the mind, a past
To mitigate the murder and disgrace
And leave him to simplicity; his last
Breath to Horatio – 'there are other worlds than this
How costly they are, yet purchased with a kiss'.

MIRANDA

It's left to you to mutter, inexpressible,
The brave new world so heartfelt and so true
With no thought of darkness reprehensible,
All will be light and growth of splendid hue,
Were you not to perish in a saga
Of soma, days of artificial heaven
When everyone dresses Lady Gaga
And people try to reckon and to leaven,
Gazettes extraordinary, beauty in nature
The daily miracle of sun and flower,
And all the taxonomy and nomenclature
Each of us a new Adam of the hour;
But yet there would be worlds still unnamed
Provided the savage Caliban be tamed.

LADY MACBETH

All the perfumes in the whole wide world,
Not to speak of Araby, or the East with all its spice
Could not sweeten my hand as these deeds unfurled
With heartless action, premonition, as a vice:
My ascent through murder is so steep
I fall off into nightmare, terror, fear
A rendezvous in Hell's caverns without sleep,
Descent into the bloody abyss, solitary and dear
That I and my flesh are doomed, a soul
Destroyed, and hell my habitation –
And so the other worlds, a whole
Lost in the fiery conflagration
Because I considered myself to be
Not a lord's, but a King's dowry.

JULIET

Your long black hair, set in a velvet bow
Your well-set shoulders tell me all I know
That you and I are no betoken age
As you take your bounding place upon my stage
So glad your grace, so lovely you of limb
That counting clans of discord does not dim
Your radiant eye, your gentleness of touch
Which show how I need you and how much
I read your looks with love in every line
Dream all night, and in your arms incline
Such gentleness and looseness all is won
Our beleaguered families need you as a sun
So much so, that you and I are all
The world needs to cleanse it of its gall.

ISABELLA

'Some rise by sin, and some by virtue fall'
I was too wise to risk eternity
And lay in proxy for the villain's call
There was no mention of paternity
Form in marriage takes a legal burden
A declaration must be with office met
Else there will be no pardon
If formality is neglected nor duty set;
Love that is limitless imposes a strict bound
And witnesses decide on couple's fate
The common destiny is of lovers found
With law and custom to be commensurate,
Lies will be uttered but truth will always out
And leave posterity no ample doubt.

HERMIONE

If her husband Leontes were indeed in love
He could see truly she was made of honour
Would not need a marble travesty, nor peace dove
To quiet his heart and give it even tenor,
Instead he whispers insults in a guest's ear
Suspects that his friend will betray him
His fevered speculation is a jealous leer
He wants nothing more than to slay him –
The queen is banished and he clears the deck
Of unattributed modesty and virtue
While she lingers by a flowery beck
Says to her daughter he will never hurt you,
Their daughter of a father whom she wins
By repentance – of her non-existent sins.

DESDEMONA

If race relations were at an all-time high
We'd have politesse and lots of love in action
Not a small-minded chief and a moon's sigh
At his most violent and un-cool reaction:
Why should a marriage founded on contrast
Yield to nonentity and a cruel trick
The quiditas of the quotidian to outlast
In a jealous rage that ignored the psychic?
So if this villain's too ambitious for his own sake,
Resorts to slander and implicates the woman
Whose whole virtue is love, just to forsake
What was to her ordinary and common –
A handkerchief, an item not pecuniary
Which needs the symbol and mores of a ceremony.

CORDELIA

Brought up on flattery, blandishment
I swore to myself a true sincerity
And my honest soul admonishment
That appearance and trumpery is not verity
When asked for love I nullified excess
Making a lowly but a true devotion
The would never perjure a success
Nor wish it something of that jade emotion
But loves dies underneath daily tribute
In small acts of service I've forsworn
I've seen honest hearts in the stocks and gibbet
And idle love vehement and lonesome
So duty calls me to deeds, not words
That lighten our souls as the air the birds.

CLEOPATRA

Not yet forgotten, though she wished oblivion
As Antony lay dead she could remember
His conquest was never a quotidian
Vial of Greek blood, Alexandria an ember
Of parchments burned as if misbegotten
The ship already like a gilded tomb
That would not perish yet; till a rotten
Extempore of dynasty in the womb
And crew who shimmied, jimmied in the mast
Made a celebration of a death, re-born
As life that was vanishing and the serpent asp
Was biting her breast until her heart was torn
And made a dark covenant of marriage vows
Indeed, eternity, the lips and brows.

SIXTY EIGHT

For years I've lived with being a *soixante-huit*er
Although my wardrobe's more fastidious and neater
Those heady days are not beyond recall
The nights and days when we first did it all
But sober work and ethics have combined
To make a settled bed my truest mind
And catalogues and dictionaries my woe
To understand what happened long ago
Far-flung days have their own allurement
But nothing beats the logic of procurement
And adventitious loves have gone the way
Of all youth, to say it's had its day
I daren't even call myself a woman sweeter –
Past perfect indiscretions tend to tweet her.

A BREATH
on the 46th anniversary of the death of Sylvia Plath, 11 February 2009

Remembering the holocaust, deep in the soonest dream
Of a beloved is buried all my hope for you begun,
So I need not wait with oil and cloves to teem
Over the mind of history, or a silver gun –
Or gas chamber with the power on
When thousands surged and left their clothes behind
Bereft of rings and ornament which shone
As the glister of a tear, shedding was too kind –
Not so bitter then, and as a lowered head
Bids goodbye, to a grim life, like the slowing eye
A candle gleam of light will haunt those dead
Who all past passing, can multitudes descry
In one poet living with expectation, thinking thrill was death
Which came, in the last sentence before your final breath.

Wild forces and wild horses held me down
Deep in the earth where the voles slumber
And nature's enemies offered a crown
To me if I help eradicate their number
Their dancing and humming all of summer
With golden suits and stripes to match
Their giddy flight and queenly hummer
Their love of the earth and ours to watch
And keep guard, like being in clover
Their golden hoard of honey and wax
Bees which were wanted on the list
Of the apothecary's potions foreign to the earth
To mint new prescriptions and poison mist
Like talc for the corn, so no plants would give birth.

A Love of Years Ago

Long years ago it was so far away
I rose up in the old morning
And watched the tide come in, play
With the seaweed that was like your hair
Brown, plentiful, and soon to fall
The boys were breasting the tide
Cold and enigmatic as your smile
That said, this is not me, nor at all
The place where our ancestors wiled
Away the hours, fished, and with a clew
Of old nets you wished you weren't you
How you felt like vanishing and fading in
The new estate, which had taken you up river
In unlikely places without maps
Where none knew you, yet a shiver
All for a dream of might be, perhaps
Yet knowing there was no going back
Not on your word, your plea, your lack
And the adamant, clear look in your eye
As you tossed your head and waved goodbye
And the tide went out and the storm in the air
Took down the leaves, but we were spared.

'ALL THIS DOING GOOD IS VERY CATHOLIC'*

He said as he sat at the wrought-iron utility desk
Beside the window whose frame was too large
'You'll get over me, you will have to risk
The transfer of love from the office to the barge
The old canal of desire in my Dutch hometown
Where we knew everything, who were the divine elect
Who saw the balance of justice He wore in the crown
Of thorns on His head, yet He was not a perfect
Father but jealous of the worship of other gods
He admits it himself, who yet is staff and rod
Everything is ordained, the elect will be saved
But some will go to Hell on the path they have paved
With good intentions', but 'I'm lacking in free will!'
'I see your progress in my view from the hill'.

* *universal*

I have not been keeping a ledger or account book
Of double entries, all the cost and price
Is not reckoned in the way you look
Or what you said, in whatever form or guise
I'll never know your motives or intentions
Whether you acted blindly or on trust
But your suspicion of all engines and inventions
Does not bury the lost meaning, or let rust

The iron will, the gold enamelling
Byzantine portraits in detail are enthralling
And with the years there comes the mellowing
Of my survivor's guilt, the clarity of my calling
It was not fair, but lust and beauty
Caused the raid, and not excise on love's duty.

APPARATCHIK CONFESSION

Underneath the grey swathe of uniform in the war zone
I scarcely detected a heart beating
If it was, it could scarcely be called my own
I had become so used to a life of cheating;
I confessed to things I hadn't done, with a curse
Dismissed the authors who had gained much fame
Saying their lack of ideology was worse
Than any traitor not worth our noble name
But someone, one of my school friends,
Had sent a live poem, infiltrated my post-box
Who had taken to writing for merely personal ends;
With me had studied ballet and eschewed bobby socks
It was not me, I swear, who ripped the poem to shreds
And threw it out of the window on the students' heads.

BIRD THOU NEVER WERT

O wild bird of my inward mind
I see you have been on the dark fantastic
Who could accuse me of being unkind
In telling the truth, you're dead with plastic
Bottle tops and caps, so bright and garish
Attracted your attention and were fatal
To your life and flight now nightmarish
The pre-figurement of the visual Babel
Scooped up, swallowed in the plastic curds
Your warning to us shows your sacrifice
As if foretelling, the augury of birds
Of humankind's intrinsic deal with dice
There's still time, thank you for the warning
Each day reckons on still another morning.

Killed: a golden-headed leader in his prime
The town becomes a by-word for assassins
The night clubs, Ruby, and a life of crime
Followed by the diet of deadly passions –
The murky depths fleshed out a tv parody
Of sex and money as a power game;
We all tuned in to this air-kiss of a threnody
How dangerous it is to have any kind of fame:
Our children schooled in years of poisoned days
Sought ways out of the constant malice
Most choked on carbon fumes in the airways
Others began to think they'd rather be like Alice –
Black holes of money – but murder stinks the palace
I tell the bereaved to blame it all on *Dallas*.

BOTH CAN'T GET JUSTICE
Ann Lovett, died in childbirth, Granard, Co. Longford, 1984, age 15

Young Ann lying in a lonely grotto
Must have sighed hard as she lay dying
Bereft of family, no religious motto
To comfort her last gasp with the baby crying

She knew a torn vessel can make of a woman
A couch-back hunched to the world's derision
Sad that this is a situation more than common
Even those who are paid to make incision

Sigh for the vessel vanquished, yet bold as thigh
On thigh, they fear all the ringed and shackled
And are not shocked as the years go by
By the casual cruelty and those heckled
Harried men who do the good other
For a woman abandoned by the brother.

DAY OF RECKONING
for the boomers

There was just so much time
From the mushroom cloud
To the wedge of doom
Where the green world lay still
As we laid the god in his tomb
In this fatal embrace
So much time to deck with grace
This last handshake of the devil
To push it down, but
We invoke Pluto as evil
Gave a dangerous substance his name
Called to the people of the world our shame
Their right to be wrong
To waste the precious song
Opportunities in some species
We became mendacious
Dealt when the god was down and out
Gave libertine professors a lot of clout
Gave people a push with their crime
Gave them conditions to develop
Their needy greedy ways to lop
All the leaves from the tree
As they die from the top
Of the world, all the bees
Wiped out with disease
All the putrid mannerisms
Of selfish dyed-in-the-wool schisms
As we lopped the trees
We didn't say please
We banged on about the private space
Thought the motor car was ace
Violated each day by the press
Who eventually flogged to death with excess
We poured our excrement into the water

Leaving no fresh springs for son or daughter
We consumed and threw away seeds
Encouraged the creation of hybrid breeds
In short we sold ourselves down the river
Our nuclear arsenals bulged in the quiver
Of our unripe exegesis of truth
Thus we squandered the planet's youth.

DOORSTOP

Keep the door closed, don't sigh as you leave
There are no tears for the hot heartache's siege
You dimmed love by; your unwillingness to grieve
Has worn the lock on this lover-liege
Who trounced you as a dunce in the classics heap
You have corralled by your attention to full stops
So there is no augury or compass to keep
Faith by; no unquenchable drinking of hops
As you in fine fettle throw letters on the fire
Kept smouldering by a scriptorium lust
As if your glazed eye would never tire
Of the millions of motes in our dust
Keep this notebook in your jar by the door
The nights since you've gone will trouble me no more.

DUSTY OLD TOWNS

In the broad sweep of the daytime world
Your flowers like trumpets dumb before the storm
As the sky throws its thunderbolts hurled
With the ageless anger like the frantic warm
Heartbeat of the god in the tumult of our blood
Shouting Awake! Awake! Everything you do matters
Never mind the is, the ought, the should
Do not destroy our earth, as dust scatters

On the wind, of pollution, CO_2 goes up
Into the air to gather dust for our lungs
While the lung of the earth, the Amazon, dries up
Until we have no music for our songs
No air, no water, no resources
For our children's children who may want to curse us.

ET TU

It wasn't for this that I left the spouse
Of innocent desire, erstwhile extravaganza
Of unvoiced tears like a hoarsened Scouse
Out for a reckless infinite bonanza;
Or to feel there was a wager in your smile
Your uncut diamond jaw of perseverance
I'd be the last to say you had the guile
For up and coming déclassé sex experience

Only that I truly loved your speech
Your rhyme and rant of justice, fortitude,
Your quelling swelling hope that each to each
Be given such a joyous plenitude;
Not that your aptness for the job of truth factotum
Was just an ageless, timeless simulacrum.

From sleeves rolled up you will cook a dinner
For me, your mother, and those who took you over
By phone call, declaring I was something of a sinner
And they were the ones to have the say, the cover
For anything you choose to name, and you grew up
Excellent at school, great on the football field
And you above all drank from the loving cup
So they in all their various pursuits did yield
To the great commandment to love. You loved indeed
Even when they took away your wild young pup
You thought it had been put down, was dead
But they heeded a final warning, not to sup
With the Devil, else face the firing squad
As Erskine Childers shook hands with his killers and
    thanked God.

FOCUS IN THE SIXTIES
i.m. Deirdre O'Connell

Through you we learned the justification of an action,
The recall of a room,
How to improvise
As we rode the night train
From Russia to America
In the sixties;
Every evening at exactly twenty to nine
Mary Elizabeth Burke Kennedy would blush on time
And Tom Hickey in his avuncular frame
Looked far into the future and the past
Peter Quince to the last
Sabina and you were sisters in *Antigone*
We saw at first hand the Greek idea
Of two rights in conflict,
You both were magnificent with
Your flowing speech and questions of conscience
Your stage glowed with these real ideas
And you were wonderful, too, in *Death of a Salesman*
I learned the American roots had more to them
Than the pop at the cinema
We saw the human being behind the stratagems
The passion behind an idea
The pull of memory
We are all bereft
For those enchanted moments
Now the rain falls gently and softly
On your parched lips and spiky eyelashes
Your hair spread like a golden mantle over your shawl
Beside your husband Luke you lie
His red curls complement your honey tresses
Bracelets of bright hair about the bone
How bright your star was, how it shone.

FOR EVEN INFINITY HAS HIS NAME

For even infinity has His name
If man or woman loving each other
Wait until perfection finds its crown –
Disinterested, like sister or brother
And making tables of the universe
When our time here is seen as thrift
To win hearts and minds, to nurse
The trying out of our perfect fit;
So why haul in the future before it's spent
A signature tune for the orchestra, bent
On seeking a permanent home while we still rent
The days widen out to unknown fulfilment,
Sure the whole universe is Goldilocks
The true, our own measure, forgetting clocks.

FOR FLESH HAS BOUNDARY, AND SPIRIT NONE

For flesh has boundary, and spirit none
So the travailed heart murmurs once again
To lift its hope along the forest run
Of wild plants drenched to their roots in rain;
So stopping by the walk amid the play
Of light and sunshine on the plants and flowers
I am brought back to that sheltering day
When you held me in your arms and all your powers
Opened to heaven like a widening door
Caressed me with the kindness of a god
That craves to love me, and more and more
Asking in tempest and with lightening rod
Why I let myself be cast down in grief,
When the beauty at my feet brings such relief.

GOD IS ALONE

The earth is filled with unrelenting pain
Our deep-down nature is a spirit void
And now we drink of poisons in the rain
With mountain majesty we have spoiled and toyed
We have brought to destruction our animals and forests
Sprayed pesticides on every kind of fruit
Paid no heed to what to the kids was dearest
Rammed a gold spoon down an acid throat
Culled our creatures filled our heads with blood
Put a price on everything that moves
Doing all we can save that what we should
All to idolise a paradigm which no one proves
Man may yet be a master of an extinct station
Out of God's loneliness we have cheated on creation.

GOLDENBRIDGE ORPHANAGE

A ring tingle of fear ran around my belly
Deep in my secret folds a spark of anger flew
To where your ears had picked up jelly –
Fish stings that wanted to be blue
It raced back to the womb of your un-desiring
Self where, abandoned, you brindled in your edge
Of razor sharp innuendo which was firing
Your awestruck envy of a child's winter knowledge
Your long arm bent my back, a spancel
Till it almost broke with the weight of zealous
Might that needs exorcism in a chancel
To make a penitent nun like you jealous
So clapped my eyes and ears that were burning
As you roasted me on the spit your ire was turning.

GOD'S GAMBLE

The self expanding to a universe
The courts of heaven peopled over time
The losers sunk in miles of rancorous verse
To a beat that attunes no one to rhyme
But without rhyme or words we would be
A different animal, a different creature
And words make things, and this is what we see
Except we love all who have a nature
God did not make robots, and for aeons we knew
Soil-soaked germinating under skies of blue
What would make us doubt His ultimate veracity
Except our blind and self-willed tenacity
Objects are strewn and float along in space
And God is there hurting at our disgrace.

No wonder they wander in the wood
Don't understand the ways of birds
Mix up the difference between shall and should
Ignore the spider in Miss Muffet's curds;
Adults screeching, living on the brink
The meaning of life is non-existence
It makes heavy thoughts for tots to think
Yet they are loved for their resistance;
Children hear the ghastly news each night
Bombs in far-off places, babies killed in strife
But worst of all their parents in a fight
The rights and wrongs of unborn siblings' life –

The cottage made of candy all too real –
The old witch – denying their right to feel.

HEART'S EASE

It might seem devilish to care
Even churlish to complain
Your perfect form wasn't made for air
But sweetens the daily dross of pain
And gives me heart's ease, an ease
That you are quite beyond compare
Like a lectern set out to tease
Even the sweetness of a misshapen pear

The lightness of thought this marries with your form
Is that moment when the universe will appease
The need for beauty, the rose before the worm
Making a world unnecessary to keys

The keenest eyes, the chilliest heart to ransom
Because you can only be described as handsome.

I had fallen, I said, out of his loving orbit
Dinners – longueurs and a little sorbet
Not a real rhyme, French not immaculate
Nor were my boyfriends highly articulate
You couldn't please him by a pretty penny
So he'd say they were just jack to my jenny
But you could say being without a dad
Brought me to the way of the multitude
And it makes me feel very sad
That I was valued only for my pulchritude
Or in the end what he said came true
My happy moments were very few
So much hurt on the day he blew
Out the candle in the dark and cried 'You!'

HOPI
for Christine Gara

You happen to have the secret of our peace
Without our logic and our logarithms
Our being, to yours, is just a tenant's lease
Of dragging feet and blotted, clotted rhythm
In your grammar is the structure of our soul
When time is just a brief imagined thing
Words like yours rest justly with the whole
Laureate which your treasures bring
The sadness that is yours today
Through our greed and thoughtlessness
Is shared by all who saw the callous way
Our ancestors deprived you, and us, of wilderness
So join with us, bereft, as we beg to ask
Forgiveness, the taking on, the putting off, the task.

I KEEP DREAMING

I keep dreaming for a final closure;
My picture in the press with condemnation
From my relatives not pleased with my exposure
To the hard-hearted cynics of the nation
To be murmured among the whole sodality
Tempered with a joke of such finesse
A stoic vision of morality
Not lacking humour in life's duress
An excommunication by the crosier
To cause in the parish consternation
And witty comments from the local hosier
To show us as a really tolerant nation
To find buried under the hub-bub is a truth
So many took the wrong turning in our youth.

I Loved You Once

Perhaps you were Orpheus, and I, Eurydice, caught
At the mouth of the cave with dreams beckoning
Afraid they will never be fulfilled, as my hand taut
In yours, slackened at that moment's reckoning:
It was only an off-chance, I cried, it was both
Yesterday and tomorrow when my heart died, random
Like a sky trail, this second, l so very loath
To touch the earth, afraid a pop-star fandom
Would fuel a worship not to last a moment,
So my wish became will, and you turned your head
To register what I was leaving, a foment
To stir the old love, with everything near dead
Your longing so great not to re-live the past
The future vanished, you were granted solitude at last.

IF LOVE'S THE WORD

If love's the word, my dictionary is sparse,
I've thought of it more times than seen the action
Not that the humour of a bedroom farce
Is worthier than another soul's attraction,
However deep I ponder on its absence
Love often hands to me a second chance
But so shy mutating into presence
It waits upon a mood, a look, a glance
And in that eye there glimmers like a light
The long distance of eternity, awake
To any possibility to make a right
Of what just seemed imaginary or fake
But real as the sand through the hourglass runs
It promises that time will send us suns.

IRON BUTTERFLY

I saw myself as I was fit to rule
The flutter-bys of any other school
With lack of care, that I was just a tool

My ordained love made functional by loss
From head to toe you bound me on a cross
As if you'd always hoped to be my boss

My hands, foresworn, were palsied with such theft
Your face was mocking, and your soul bereft
You called another's name where I was cleft;

I try to mend with sweetly evoked rhyme
And love on celluloid, whose song is mine
As if every frenzy were a love divine

To know no other but this dream of day
To place you in my arms, so much my clay
As if no better life, no other way

This love of mine was lost before you came
Shows how you borrowed off my dearest claim
He cannot breathe or cannot say my name
Who robbed me of my goodness has no fame.

IS THERE ONE WHO UNDERSTANDS ME?*

* James Joyce's last words

Death is such a soft word, it cleaves
To the tongue, the life, the title, the work
Of the father, whose bolus, wet flowering leaves
Becomes an acrid heap upon a mother's look –
Her hair soft on his pillow to lurk
Where a tonsured head might gleam
Like a small candle's glow and spark
Her accent soft as a red fruit dream
An unfinished chapter in an adventure book
Like a promise given to overlook
Such things as brought her to a birth-room swoon
In his garrotting of an apostle head on a spoon
Views tempered with a stolen memory, a key
To lips, adhered to – goodbye too soon.

JANUS

January opens its portals with a timid eye
In our efforts to understand who bear the brunt
When the gatekeeper hears the cruel hunt
Of a hawk upon a sparrow, the emboldened cry

Of what excites and violates the good.
In the making of a counterpane a dropped stitch
A random pecking of disorder should
Make the real tangible, the real rich

But to lace with vent open in the breast
What's stopped has started the outward flow
Where the eye has fled to stumble after rest
The shut pupil now must now inward go:
Beauty is extreme order arrived at by accident,
Loved in the Orient. Shattered in the Occident.

MAD IRELAND HURT ME, TOO

Mad Ireland hurt me too, that fecund race
Crazy with love and jealousy and both
Craven and haughty, yet bowing to a mace
And tinkering with a class so like, so loath
Captains and slaves, warriors and bards
Rhymesters exact with consonant and vowel
Curses and blessings, crosiers and cards
Afflictions from the head unto the bowel
A melange, a mixture yet a straitened crew
Of attachment, probity and learning
Seeing both opposite and apposite as true
Blind, yet visionary in its impetuous yearning:
Blood, and the honeysuckle bower
The red rose, and the lily in one hour.

My Good Days and my Bad Days

I have my good days and my bad days
Eros has trimmed his brows somewhat
Setting off to some far-distant land in a haze
Trailing over the side of the boat his worn love-knot.
Prejudice sits quietly on my window sill
It's hard to forget and hard to remember
How he lit up my days so much I could fill
A cornucopia with fruits in this mild December
Now he's definitely gone, his last plea
You'll regret this, a net over his shoulder
I'll leave you to your reminiscences and your tea
As you gradually grow older and older
Remember, I left you with a loving child
To gladden your heart on your return from the wild.

Nightjar

At times I'm one who listens to the night
The twitching silence by the berry bush
The snap of twigs and wires that are too tight
The sudden turbulence of sweet green rush
Like the way you pitch your shoulder at the past
The airs you've given to deny a bond
The least you do wants to be the last
To praise an honest heart that's still too fond
Of hunkering in the dark till the singing of the lark
Lest growing fears make reprisal for those deeds
Even the noise of keys that rattle in the dark
Is brought to daylight, like all the weeds
And thoughts of you, and withered witcheries that try
At times to blot out in the day my truthful eye.

NOTE TO THE PATRIARCH

I crossed the Rubicon for you, made sport
Of Latin masters in a weft embargo
I waited for the troops while your retort
Gave contretemps of destiny's bright cargo
I leaned my ear to pavement's pounding feet
To hear your clarion call from high above
I looked out to the west and to the east
And the name of everything was love;

Still you estimated me as weak
My character held up by lamp-lit maps
As if I were a harbinger to wreak
Havoc on the heads of love's young saps
I didn't count your ego as my loss
Until you had me tied upon the cross.

Tell me what divine creature lodged in your house
Under the counterpane, a spirit who knows
The difference between an elephant and a mouse
And in what direction the wind blows
And those sweets made of artificial vegetable oil
Which you flung back on the proof of ages
Who in the indeterminate college will spoil
Such Herculean labours of the sages?
To render all fit for the epigram of taste
Good food to the mind's questing daze
Or apothegms to heap onto your praise
Like all the questions you haven't faced
Which year upon tears, tears after years before
Would have brought you to another hallowed door.

OUR FRIEND AND POET TOM MOORE

*On the occasion of the visit of the Irish Byron Society to the grave
of Tom Moore at Bromham, Wiltshire, October 2011*

You brought such harmony to heart and head
Two civilizations met as equal,
You set the tone for years when living and dead
Gave to your haunting need for peace a sequel;
The fragile moments of a nation's history
Were caught by you to furnish us with song,
You faced the spirit wound of so much mystery
To heal ourselves of the centuries' wrong,
Yet found a twin soul, a friend and brother
One like you, outcast upon fate
And learned to love each country like no other
Made of Irish and English an unlikely mate:
We celebrate the rich gems of your ore
Set in this culture, honouring Byron and Moore.

REMOTE CONTROL

He still haunts me, his sour invective
Chills my sprouting thoughts of lambent ease
I should have really hired a detective
To log forensically his mind's striptease
But they were wrong who hampered my footfall
As if my broken mind was theirs to see
To stand and deliver a witch's call
To bury all my hopes under a polluted sea
Two vigilantes coifed for an appraisal
Their own mudguard seems stuck to the ground
Till daubing paint in blobs upon an easel
Was the pure, purest delight I ever found
And as a necklace ties one like a garrotte
Is stuffed to the gills like a dead stolen parrot.

STAGE FRIGHT

Stub-toed in the alien porn, in our endeavour
To be godlike, in forgetting shake shank morbidity
So that we deny the earth-bound a fervour
Of Valhalla mud in our rapidity
To make and adore idols, anything we created
To fall down and worship before, save our true Maker
And by a tunnel versioned self directed
All but the most sublime, disconnected shaker
All green hills subside to slides of mud
All trees have roots to ward us of this pain
All seas congeal with chemicals and blood
Acidic waters give us cancerous rain
True to our mad muddiness, mouths filled with earth
A wind jammer in the cornices, blowing fine our girth.

STALINGRAD 1942*

None of them would be worth it if it was your son
The nameless soldiers killed in Stalingrad
To one we had to whisper their names one by one
And say for each death, we are but glad
It wasn't us, or yours, or mine
It wasn't someone we had grown up with
Some we had loved as a grape the vine
Someone we knew for the heart's core and pith
Not even a face on a photo frame
Seeking an exploratory thumb, a breath caught swift
At recognition that somehow news and fame
Had stopped short in a histrionic shift
Erasing claim and name, even number
The bones unclassified, now burnt to umber.

The year I was born in Dublin

THANKS FOR YOUR GREEN ACTIONS

I haven't felt it very much this year
The closing in of night in shorter hours
The clock does not watch in blinkered fear
But quietly keeps what is mine and ours
Gentle agreement that the past was gone
Once embedded like a lectern in a hall
Now with our peace of radiance shone
Your actions – we were the victors after all
The time spent was fruitful its slow ease
Into night and dark does not hurt so much
As was your silence holding out to tease
At times yielding to my gentler touch
Now at the turn of year the days are bright
Once more I keep your picture in my sight.

THE BIRD WAS NOT MYTHICAL

If my father found a bird with a broken wing
Something which I find to be truly mystical
He'd put the bird under his jacket to bring
Home to our house, where it would sing and sing

And my father played music – he was not typical
Though the urban cowboys declared him risible
A man who cared, more than just physical
I thought he was the once and future king

With pain and joy for each natural thing
Unknown to all who like fake sparkle and bling
And tuneless tunes that are far from lyrical
But the birdsong is the most important thing

And the bird was free to sing, so spiritual
– it was a real bird, not merely mythical
A song for his mending and perfect wing
That he be free to fly and sing and sing

A song divine of which he is the vehicle
More than a blessing, a life to ring
Around our hearts: a thanks for everything.

It was not for this you took me on the whirligig
Tour of the senses, the deliberate synaesthesia
Where emotion turned to colour in a rainbow jig
And danced until I dropped death of kinaesthesia
No, it was the deliberate dismantling
Of the character that skirted borders of crime
And illegal speakeasies where the fatling
Of surcease and luxury wasted all our time
The clampers on the hamper, the fathomless jibes
The undercurrent sextant of the galaxies
Where you rotated all the culture of the tribes
To pin Minerva as the chief among the doxies
You nearly killed me, your cynicism and fever
Touted and sold me, all my faith and fervour.

THE DESOLATE HARBOUR

Hurt and harm, the masts are lying low
On boats called 'Careless' and the plodding tug,
There is no sea deep enough to show
My loss of you, who never had a hug
Or even if you did have a thought
It lay unexpressed in your forming brain
As I with love and life besought
My lover in the unrelenting rain;
But this is Ireland, such things never happen
As brought to grief and desolation
The church bell tolled on it misshapen
Interlude of lust and fornication
Our love was true, though promised to another
A legal fiction caused this needless slaughter.

The world was magical years before I was born
Testament of the natural world in bygone days,
But Big Pharma's poisons came to haze the corn
The big flowers of summer's gorgeous ways
Neonicotinoids to kill the bee population
To hold back blooms until they were only a memory
Like the glass flowers of the poet's adulation
And once-bright wings which were a shimmery
Murmur of your breathing in your sleep
And the quiet movement of the moon
Above the trees with leaves so deep
Green they were the sorcerer's boon
Like you they were born not too soon
But not too late, there's still time
To call on to Big Pharma to confess the crime.

THE GHOST OF SHELLEY AT LERICI, 1963

The slow kindling light, the dash of the sea
Against the shoreline, as if your storied death
Of hopes and dreams were everything to be;
Somehow in the vapour of the night's breath
Your face comes to me, and your willow neck
Bowing to the imperatives of your misspent youth
That broken trust, of those that would dissect
The tales and motives of your unvarnished truth
Of Nature's love and beauty in the day –
It was certain that it was never-ending
Yet the demise of you, and the ancient way
In breaking, a crude science was now unbending
Yet, with the light, your memories keep in store
And gladden my own days with tints of ever more.

The groves of learning are hot-beds of reverie
Exotic blooms on a fact-finding mission
A deal with the devil of memory
Debate between nuclear fusion and fission;
Wall to wall laments of ages past
Red plastic pliers deep into the skull
Waiting rooms of rectitude none can lambast
Until the nightly grog grows to empty from full;

Running along the fine stitching the broad strokes of fear
That catapult daydreams of another place
Using what cannot be used, a sudden tear
Falling so beautifully down a pilgrim face
Kiss away, kiss away for the certitude
That you are the leaven in the multitude.

I didn't want to abandon to the portico
Or the drawbridge with its dizzy height
Your keeling over the chaos of watershed below
I didn't see how far you'd come bright
As the oozing lamp behind the lattice
Of your desire, how far I'd gone
To the ends of the earth making a poultice
For your severed arm, your blue breastbone
Hitting your back ribs as if you hadn't got a heart
When I believed your words of sympathy and sanction
No one could cast a stone, a question dart
At you, spellbound at the auction
Of your dark secrets, your travestied gaze
Upon the spilled honeycomb of our wasted days.

Perched on the windowsill and betrayed twice over
The flapper let caution go with the wind
Which had jammed her hand on her hat on her hair
As she was climbing to the lintel
Where she had forsaken her calling,
And bending, cried into the letterbox
My pages have disappeared with the morning
Sun and now lie scattered
In some deep shade of longing
Open to the wind and rain
The kind that lives within a summer breeze
And a sudden shower
Which catches the heart in a
Beautiful kind delight.
Nobody heard her,
But she was sure someone or something
Deep in the cosmos had changed its essence
Rather than let her prayer go to waste.

THE LOST HEMI-CYCLE OF WOMEN'S WORK

In the pasture land of never-never, your
Broom-tilted scavenging of the archive,
Ready to make all domestic, pure
As the rage you translated live;
Arraignments of taste bedecked your bucolic
Adventures in skin and bone; petals pink
And red spelled romantic reasons, think
Of a heavy army winter overcoat, your frolic
Over the airways, you said, why sample
The dead-ends, the never do wells,
We are a generation of example
Working with doctrine and with magic spells
To sweep up the leavings under our collars
Our last refuge is a redemption for scholars.

The poetry of love is never dead
It will shine out, like on a dark night
The moon falls onto a glistening head
Or a rain-washed pavement with a bead of light
So your voice, once true and loud
Now whispers of your life's sad disappointments
With the motives attending desire in a crowd
Of broken promises and missed appointments;
Still there is one who loves you like a child
Looking at an endless infinity of hope
And love and desire, and friendship mild
As a languid hand staying the rope
Like pearls on my neck, each one counting the cost
Of lover never kissed, nor person lost.

THE PRIMROSE PATH

The primrose path to hell is now a highway
All nature's herbs are tight sealed up in plastic;
As men and women try to do it 'my way'
Even to the point of acts quite drastic
Swinging from the chandeliers mundane
As lace and glass come crashing on the bed
Leaving a corpse that's waked all night with henbane
And, through a conversation left unsaid
Such as I really meant it all to last,
But, giddy with the light of my adventure
We got into things far too fast
And now we're steeped in debt and in debenture
Not to speak of the plastic island in the ocean:
All because of your emotionless commotion.

THE SADDEST DAY

It was Christmas around nineteen eighty
The child was clutching Dad's five pound voucher
He had nothing on his mind more weighty
There was a knock on the door, the social worker
Who was a friend came over on the bus
Santa was busy and said next please
It was clear the child wasn't one of us
And that Christmas was a giant big tease

The social worker lost the piece of paper, the disguise
Of Santa was annoyed there might be a refund
His office was a plastic cave with plastic skies
And the population for him were far too fecund
I wished I had the wherewithal to buy the child a racer
To tear through the house, so he no longer had to face her.

THE TIGER POEM

Majestic creature of the virgin era
Proud but energized to pounce
Show to all who fear you
Humankind is a wayward dunce
Keep your brightness for tomorrow
Let your glory shine for us
When we forget this present sorrow
How we thought you just a puss
You belong to him who made you
You belong to the ancient earth
As we hurtle from this dark age
Into one when we have rebirth
Thank you for your grace
Thank you for your glory
Hope you're with us in the future
To have with us a better story.

THE TROUBLE IS WE DON'T LOOK ALL THE SAME

The male advances many women dread
Cause others to make nudity the norm
Some would rather be mortgaged to a bed
Than have an exhibition of their female form;
Suicide is commonly called *felo de se*
A crime of oneself against the person.
The public confession and burning of works is *auto da fe*
And the burning of buildings is called arson
I hear the Danes wore yellow stars
So not to point out who were Jews,
Presidents only travel in black state cars
And a *burqua* a *djellaba* can refuse
Words are important, even rest on a comma
None of us born targets for a bomber.

Paper trails have logged my journey
As an ongoing faith healer type of recusant
Who ends up on the hospital gurney
Being revived with details no reticent
Chronicler can part with or convey –
What happens in the micro-management blog
Is a tortured reflection of the way
Everything points in the ensuing fog
To right and wrong like a sharp cry
Of a battered baby brought to destruction
Because no one knew enough to ask why
When she was turned away from the bridal auction
A tear in her eye for what she had lost
The years of happiness, the terrible cost.

There are few times more precious than the play's whirligig
When nurturing is needed on the night slopes of sleep
To let regret pall from its ruddy tumbling jig:
The dance has ended, there is more to keep
The memory of your faltering steps away
How they rebounded in a quick return
Back to my heart where you sing all day
Hardly noticing the leaves that burn
In small courtyards where the past is raked
Over and over for your lost first shoes
When she took away the good with her faked
Affection, nothing to give to me and you
But her false love, kept under her pillow
While tears lapped lakes at the foot of the willow.

THERE'S NO ART
   ... to find the mind's construction in the face (Shakespeare)

Sometimes a harried face can enthral
As if stamped with the courage of adventure
Its deep pocks and ridges show the squall
Your soul buffeted and bartered in indenture
Your brass locks, the tuft behind you eye
The scar where he threw you down the stair
Though you did not pucker your mouth in a cry
But hunched your shoulder and let loose a prayer
How devious are the ways of adversity
Columns were written by the mascara that ran
Like a blackened trail in a horny city
That led to the TV and newspaper scan
Your story is written, and in your face
Is the augury of how well you bear disgrace.

THROWN BY A TRYST

Coming from fields where once the bard meandered
To squire a topless model of existence
In a nonfeasance of a body too much wandered
In the trite purlieus of your staid resistance;
A splash of colour was needed for your song
Provided it was raucous bright, and red
To put on a banner that was waved too long
Before it collapsed, stricken, by a bed

A hold of tight emotions in a picket
No pocket in this traveller's suit of woe
That ended up stretched upon a thicket
Open to the rains of long ago
Who will rescue the rags of promises now torn
Long before you and I were born?

TO THE IRISH BARDS AND REVIEWERS

A cryptic pseudo-myth, a gnomic trail
Has sent the bards of Éireann on a rail
To spoof the Pangur Bán electric cat
With homonyms of bleary waitroom chat
While telling bees about it is the answer
Because only they can know the cure for cancer
Old pilgrim trails in holy wells and grottos
Furnish the hierophantic world with mottoes
Away a glitch on a computer virus
Will finally find us out, and even tire us
But keep the jottings and the notebooks clean
We'll dazzle you with what engine searches glean,
To daft the memory and make holes in space
Which celebrate the glory of our race.

TO SEAMUS HEANEY ON HIS 70TH BIRTHDAY

Not for you the night-time deeds of fate,
Which stow in the heart the shadows of late-
Developing deadly osmosis, yet to hear
A quiet tenor sigh, see a slow-falling tear
On the crumpled leaf of bogwood
As the tarred maiden drank wormwood
The scarcely breathable hope and history –
Such stuff to decry the archaic mystery:
Enlivened now, the god of the good sounds, no quack
Of the bronze urn or 'earth-somnolent' coffee claque
But hearing the auditory gurgle of the motor car
Being there, knee-deep in the river, and far
Into the grass, to follow the track of horse and hare
Show us your exemplary love and care.

TRUST BROKEN

There's not someone who hasn't felt that way
Clouded in a brooding moment with a sad
Heavy lurch of the heart to gainsay
Anything that could be misconstrued as bad
Like the time she felt somehow he had strayed
A lull, a silence on the telephone
An intake of breath, a smile arrayed
Then swiftly extinguished like a xylophone

A cacophonous sound before being put away
A drawer stuck, a smidgen in the eye
A trust broken, what more is there to say
A silence that endured past by the by
A quilt upturned, a pillow smashed in rage
The putting on of mask, a life on stage.

WAYWARD SISTER

Damned by desuetude, the brother harkens
To the childhood nomenclature for his sister
When he thinks of her his heart darkens
The sputum on his lips curls to a blister
Her name did not help, it was of a flower
Now he names her, shames her, frames her
Their childhood games have shown a gendered sour
Gloss, and swept, lost, are those who claim her
Not for her virtue, intelligence or pride
A purity and goodness of heart
But that she will never be at his side –
She has chosen for herself her art
He has the right of all those born to favour
Will his loyalty to patriarchy ever waver?

WHERE WERE WE?

Saying more than I intended
Bread delicious! Movie great!
I thought of how you and I contended
I with my shadow, you with a likely mate
Fictitious accounts can never be clear
As real women are not wanted now
The floodgates of pornography cost dear
We are either or a goddess or a cow
Should you declare your orientation
Is something more than turning to the East
And its fans and jars a lamentation
Of beauty in a culture more discreet
Can we be both, can we be either?
We both know the horse has lost its rider.

WALKING THE TALK

Cars guzzle petrol, are not green
Yet outside meetings still are seen
'Next week, next year, we'll take the bus
As long as it will not inconvenience us'.
'The Dart doesn't come to my area
Walking alone at night would scare ya'
'Of course I'm far too important
To worry about the odd asphyxiant'.
'I've simply got to get to where
They're having a meeting on clean air'
'I'd like to save resources like metal
And couldn't tread upon a petal'
'They'll find more oil, wait and see
The grand-children, fiddle dee dee'.
All day long in a parking lot
The wealth of tomorrow starts to rot
The real cost of the motor car
Is borne by kids, and carried far
Are fumes and downward economics
For someone else's bag of tricks
Share – if you have one – you must
Lest your good intentions gather dust
Make sure your exhaust is immaculate
To make your protests heard articulate
Heave yourself on to a bus
Become, in fact, one of us,
These combined with use of taxis
Is a noble form of praxis
Example is by far the best teacher
Practice is what saves the preacher.

ZERO LOVER

You crush me with your platitudes of scorn
And run in competition with my hero
As if winning silver cups since you were born
Qualifies you to be a more than zero
Your education wasted as you thrive on norms
It would fill a rockery with your kisses
Not counting all your conquests made in dorms
Where princesses cite out loud their near near-misses
You scored on empathy when not a note
In your wildest range can make a register
You learn the newspapers by rote
Apply to the prima donna as a chorister
In sum you try too hard to find gut feeling
Your emotional range a tadpole on the ceiling.

THE WRONG LETTER

Why did it have to happen in the end?
The day propitious as the morning sun
The letter which declared you were my friend
And would be so the length of life's long run
A suicide bid, two breakdowns, and a ton
Of excuses a whisperer might lend
To teasing kin to say it was all in fun
Why did it have to happen in the end?
It felt so passionless, a word to send
To all lovers that all hope was gone
A meaning that no sage could twist and bend
A day propitious as a morning sun
Now disappointments, all delight would shun
Each page of the letter I would rend
As dismal import of a jealous nun
The letter which declared you were my friend
Read cold, it had quite transfixed a pun
On life, on meaning, squeezing what you'd penned
To read just like a firing from a gun
And so it shattered thus my life's long run
Now, through my window all the hills look dun
Gone is their green, my saviour lone to tend
A strong desire for wisdom has been won
For nothing's clear but for my life to mend
Why did it have to happen?

FOR THOMAS CHATTERTON

A dying age can auction anything
A gift unasked for is a lease on truth
A tiger's eye is what a god can fling

On knowing nothing You can invent the zing
Of medieval manuscript, marvellous youth!
A tender age will rescue everything

The robes of angels merely wring
Out of infinity. Exiled Ruth
Saw in tiger's eye a star of sing,

Cornfields were her transept, songs to ring
Out of otherness, but your scrivener's sleuth
Makes purloined sage, and forgery your king

Your own is your own, remember Charity can bring
Every lonely outcast to the raging tooth
Where tiger's eye remembers envy's sting

Exact a reply. So out of pain, spring
Love's pride, however raw, uncouth,
Are not imitations, but sage, your own, your wing,
Be tiger's eye, you butterfly of sing.

When the bridge has been cast adrift
When all the marks and traces of our rift
Mock with languor all for which you sighed
In the howling storm outside,
You will be in a stranger zone
Unable to articulate what is your own
In this land whose tenure is late –
No longer seeing the torrent in spate
Or ruins crumbling. But green shoots
Where once doom had put down roots
A new civilisation wanders
Now you are sufficient to what renders –
You cannot see what has gone before
The broken jetty of reason
Swings over like an open door
And you can cry of a new season
As first love lies beyond your ken
While each kiss can resurrect
The beauty of your vanished Zen
And universal kindness, as a sect
Flourishes now, where once was dust
Ancient memories have grown blind
You can have them if you must –
But all will be recovered, all are sparing
Of difference and distance not yet signed
With this rebirth comes a new sharing,
Leaving agonies of youth behind.

An Overdue Letter to Lord Byron

Written to celebrate Lord Byron's Birthday, 22 January 2013, and on the discovery that my ancestor Rear-Admiral Joshua Rowley fought along with Byron's grandfather Admiral John Byron at the battle of St Lucia, Granada in February 1779

1

If fetters were the king of all captivity
I'd be bound and frozen in my station
Just as the method of receptivity
Confines the giver's art on some occasion;
I'll warrant that you had a time with levity
And added to the gaiety of the nation
Those callipers which bound your leg were vain
At every turn you rose against the pain.

2

There's many a country lost because a tragic
View of life makes suffering unconditional
Almost compulsory, like a haemorrhagic
Outpouring of blood that's not medicinal
I'd rather take to fairy tales and magic
Than waste another life on hate perditional
As the poet Yeats has made of our new nation
A fairyland with an ultimate dispensation.

3

If bards were to govern all our history
We'd have tales supernatural by the dozen
An endless mesmeric of shifting mystery
That ends up in a proposal to a cousin;
Now, with gangs and robbery and bistoury
If only these chains of affliction we could loosen
And make among ourselves a peaceful state
Independent of what we did and didn't ate.

4

Forgiving is the best of Christian virtue
All who have offended given pardon
Felicitations received from those who hurt you
Epistolary hortatory poems by Auden
And by scholars worldwide you have your due
More prolific than an herbaceous garden
So multifarious has been your praise
It outnumbers your fans and lovers, it's a craze.

5

They talk of towns and cities now are twinning
The wild impulses which are so romantic
Performance, number, beauty all are spinning
Through a revolving door of moods so frantic
It seems that biography over verse is winning
Readers who love to read of tryst and antic
If all these populations were like Byron
They'd break each and every note they tried a lyre on.

6

They say you are the father of modernity
The first found to be famous overnight
The first swooning-by celebrity
And everything else described as modern blight
They say you are a wicked confraternity
But your bark is more tremendous than your bite
In short, you cut such a dashing figure
It causes multitudes to swoon, and some to snigger.

7

Some say such work is just a crafty drivel
While others moan about its bad prolixity
Still others indicate a haughty swivel
From the chairman who applauds its swift dexterity
Which dazzles as a naughty nifty bevel
In a mirror indicates its true capacity
While others cite the knickers on the floor
Without calculation for the stricken poor.

8

If there could be countless Caesered Romes
A rubric to become a strutting pigeon
What if the falling off in frenzied domes
A boyish catapult thrown at religion
All believers sentenced to the tomes
Of history's blandishments not worth a squidgen
All revels to the grave end in a fever
If a woman talks there's no one would believe her.

9

In vain the wishes of an angry crowd
Expel with air a live aristocrat
Why punish one who caterwauls out loud
Exemplar of a fine articulated fiat
Or move the tenor of a head now bowed
Until it ends in final caveat
To go unarmed on to the guillotine
Exerting right until Don Juan bursts their spleen.

10

And beauty has a role in each observer
It inches up the face until the eyes
Blink with the blindness of one of those who serve her
The muse is taken with a charming guise
And will not take payment for a waiver
Never to hold on to history's lies
By such stratagem Don Juan evades the noose
When he finds he has a talent to amuse.

11

I wonder if you are such a bad influence
You bring much merriment after supper
That isn't one who doesn't smile at the confluence
Of wit and wisdom on the up and upper
In times of penury following affluence
To hear such a prodigious, prolific author
Our human foibles and frailties laid bare
As presumably your going naked up a stair.

12

But what I want to say your generosity
Of spirit, plenitude, and purse
Giving us such serendipitous virtuosity
To take away from all affliction any curse
Your benign good will, your learned curiosity
Your latitude and wit which you disperse
Into magniloquence that's hardly terse,
Your mighty opus is our universe.

ONE LOVE – A WEDDING SONNET 2012

For my son David and his wife Siobhán

One love is needed to set us up in life
One true person we can really trust
As loving husband and as loving wife
A friendship and a faithful heart a must

Through the years to come we wish you joy
Whatever comes to you we'll celebrate
The union of a lovely girl and boy
Lucky enough to find the perfect mate

With liking and respect now well proven
Try on the wedding rings, a perfect fit
As your life threads together are woven
You'll read the book of love which long ago was writ

Especially for you both on your wedding day
We join with you in a love that will surely stay.

'Lyrics of a rare strength and delicacy'

– John McGahern

'I like the poems ... I keep hearing something in them
that I'm always listening for ... and rarely catch'

– Ted Hughes

'Originality, commitment, and real literary ability'

– Eiléan Ní Chuilleanáin

'Her range of vocabulary and phrasing is impressive ...
a true poet ... her finest poems wear their learning
lightly – she excels as a critic'

– Declan Kiberd

'A master of form'

– Brendan Kennelly

'Her voice is one of heart-breaking beauty'

– Roz Cowman

'100% improvement on Christina Rossetti'

– Geoffrey Thurley

'I have listened to *Flight into Reality* with a lot of
pleasure ... I think it is quite beautiful and very
thought-provoking'

– Brendan Glacken

Rosemarie Rowley, born in Dublin in 1942, has written extensively in form, including terza rima, rhyme royal and rhyming couplets. She is a four times winner of the Epic Award in the Scottish International Open Poetry Competition. She has degrees in Irish and English Literature, and philosophy from Trinity College Dublin, an M.Litt on the nature poet Patrick Kavanagh, and a diploma in psychology from the National University of Ireland. She has been active in the green movement in Ireland and in the Irish Byron Society and worked for a time in the European institutions in Europe. She has given papers for academic conferences in Ireland, the UK, the USA and several universities on the European mainland.

Also by Rosemarie Rowley:

The Broken Pledge (Dublin, Martello, 1985)
The Sea of Affliction (Dublin, Comark, Rowan Tree, 1987)
Politry (Dublin, Rowan Tree Press, 1988)
Flight into Reality (Rowan Tree Press, 1989)
Hot Cinquefoil Star (Dublin, Rowan Tree Press, 2002)
In Memory of Her (Dublin, Rowan Tree Press, 2008)

www.rosemarierowley.ie